Comfort in times of Sorrow

Scripture taken from the New King James Version. Copyright © 1982 by
Thomas Nelson, Inc. Used by permission. All rights reserved.

© Roger Carswell 2003

ISBN 1-85792-895-4
ISBN 978-1-85792-895-2

Published in 2003,
reprinted in 2004 and 2007
by
Christian Focus Publications, Ltd.,
Geanies House, Fearn, Ross-shire,
IV20 1TW, Scotland, UK

www.christianfocus.com

Cover design by Alister MacInnes

Printed and bound by
Bell & Bain, Glasgow

Comfort in times of Sorrow
by Roger Carswell

Imagine you are standing on a seashore. A sailing ship is at your side spreading her white sails to the morning breeze as she sets sail for the ocean. The ship looks beautiful and strong. You watch her until eventually she seems like a speck of white cloud just where the sea and sky meet each other. Someone at your side says, "There, she's gone."

But where has she gone? Gone from your sight, that's all. She is just as large in mast and hull as she was when she left the shore. She is still carrying her load of living weights to its destination. Just at the moment when someone says, "She's gone" another voice on a distant shore shouts, "She's here!".*

Death is similar. Earth's loss is eternity's gain. Each one of us has an endless existence, first in this world, and then in the next.

The Christian is certain that when he or she is "absent from the body", they are immediately "present with the Lord".

---

* Based on a Victor Hugo idea.

3

Nevertheless, there is no emotion so deeply distressing as grief. The death of a loved one leads to sadness, shock, numbness, and bewilderment. Feelings of regret, guilt, anger and self-pity surface, as memories emerge. Some of these recollections are intensely happy; others are painful. But the sense of loss lingers.

Thank God for the ability to shed tears, but it can feel that an ocean full will not be enough to heal the hurt.

Endless words from family and friends are well meaning but inadequate to relieve the heartache and heaviness of the loss. Nevertheless, people want to genuinely sympathise in your sadness.

There is comfort

Who then can help us at such a time? Where can genuine comfort be found? Not in social life, nor in solitude; not in the stars or spiritism, but in the Saviour. The Bible says, "Blessed be the God and Father of our Lord Jesus Christ, the Father of mercies and God of all comfort, who comforts us…" God cares for us, can cope with us and will comfort us in our deepest distress, if we turn to Him and trust Him. God, in the Bible, promises:

> "When you pass through the waters, I will be with you; and through the rivers, they shall not overflow you.
> When you walk through the fire, you shall not be burned, nor shall the flame scorch you.
> For I am the Lord your God" (Isaiah 43:2-3).

There is comfort in knowing that God has Himself suffered grief over the death of a loved one, and therefore understands how we feel, and sympathises in all our sorrows.

God's one and only Son, the Lord Jesus, came from heaven to suffer the horrible death of execution on a Roman cross. Jesus was born for that episode in His life. It was during the hours on the cross that Jesus actually paid the price of our sin. He died the death of us all, for He was carrying the penalty of all our wrongdoing, to buy forgiveness for us, if only we will trust Him. God is just, and must punish wrongdoing, but Christ has died in our place and taken the judgment which should be ours. Such is God's love to each of us.

There is comfort in knowing that Jesus has overcome death by rising again from the dead. He is the One who has come back from the dead and has told us of life after death. Death has been defeated. It is not the end. For all who are trusting in Christ as their personal Saviour, it is the doorway to eternal life in heaven.

There is comfort in knowing that God promises to never leave us nor forsake us once we have put our trust in Him.

There is comfort in knowing that God is willing to forgive us for all our wrongdoing, if by faith we call upon Him.

Death is not the end. God the Maker of heaven and earth, and the Giver of life, has told us in His Word, the Bible, that there is life after death:

"You will show me the path of life; in Your presence is fullness of joy; at your right hand are pleasures for evermore" (Psalm 16:11).

"Jesus said, 'I am the resurrection and the life. He who believes in Me, though he may die, he shall live'" (John 11:25).

"Our Saviour Jesus Christ, who has abolished death and brought life and immortality to light through the gospel" (2 Timothy 1:10).

"For God so loved the world that He gave His only begotten Son, that whoever believes in Him should not perish but have everlasting life" (John 3:16).

In some ways it could be a daunting thought that God knows the secrets of the hearts and lives of all men and women. After death, each individual will stand before Him, and then it will be impossible to hide anything from Him.

Lord Hailsham, a previous Lord Chancellor said, "When I die and stand before God in judgement, I will plead guilty and cast myself upon the mercy of the court." How wise of him!

The Bible teaches that there is both heaven and hell: a place of bliss and a place of banishment. They are for eternity. None of us deserves heaven; we are simply not good enough. However, we need not be frightened. Psalm 23 has classic Bible words:

"Yea, though I walk through the valley of the shadow of death, I will fear no evil for You (God) are with me" (Psalm 23:4).

It is possible to be absolutely certain of a place in heaven, through trusting the Lord Jesus.

Our sins (wrong thinking, speaking and doing) separate us from God. The Bible teaches that it is our sin which is the sting of death. Wondering how our lives will be looked on and how we will fare when it comes to life after death can be troubling issues. It is normal to ask if after life we will see our loved ones again. Deep down we know that it is not true that we've "never done anything wrong". All of us have sinned. How will all this affect us? How can one be sure of heaven?

Christ came to pay the price of our wrong attitudes and actions. The Bible says,

> "There is... no condemnation to those who are in Christ Jesus" (Romans 8:1).

A family was having a picnic in the Yorkshire Dales, when suddenly the seven-year-old girl began to panic. A bee was flying near her and she, tightly shutting her eyes, was petrified. Quickly her father stood up and swiped away the bee. As he did, it stuck to him, stung him, shook itself and flew away free. Turning to his daughter and reassuring her said, "You're all right now. A bee can only sting once, and I have taken the sting." Similarly, Christ in His death on the cross took the sting of death – our sin – on Himself as He died. We can be safe for eternity, because of Jesus.

Not only did He die once and for all, but rose again from the dead once and for all. He has conquered death. The living Christ promises His presence in life, through death and for all eternity. This is how the Bible describes heaven:

"I saw a new heaven and a new earth … And I heard a loud voice from heaven saying, 'Behold, the tabernacle of God is with men, and He will dwell with them, and they shall be His people. God Himself will be with them and be their God. And God will wipe away every tear from their eyes; there shall be no more death, nor sorrow; nor crying. There shall be no more pain, for the former things have passed away" (Revelation 21:1-4).

It is normal and natural to grieve. However, even at this time of sorrow, God can draw near to you to strengthen and help you. Simply ask Him in prayer. Ask Him to become your Friend and Comforter, your Lord and Saviour. He will be with you through every season of your life. His presence will sustain you in difficult and joyful times. He is not merely a crutch in tough times, but a constant Friend. When eventually death comes to you, its devastating power will have been broken because of the Lord Jesus.

A well-known gospel preacher was returning with his children from the funeral service of his wife. He wondered what to say to comfort his motherless children. Just then, a huge moving lorry passed them, casting its shadow over the car. Inspiration came, and the father asked his children, "Children, would you rather be run over by a truck or by its shadow?" The answer was clear. Then he said, "Did you know that two thousand years ago the lorry of death ran over the Lord Jesus in order that only its shadow might run over us?"

You may find these words helpful to pray, asking God to bring you into a living relationship with Himself.

Dear God, thank you that you understand all my feelings. You know that there is so much in life that I regret, and I am sorry for all that is wrong. Thank you for your love. Thank you that Christ died for me. Thank you that He rose from the dead. Please forgive me, and come to live in my life as my personal Lord, Saviour and Friend. Comfort me at this time, I pray, in Jesus' name. Amen.

Conclusion

In times of sorrow, it is good to know that God, who made heaven and earth, has spoken to all humanity through His Word, the Bible. I would recommend systematically reading a chapter or so of the Bible, day by day. Perhaps you could start with the Gospel of John. You will see how Jesus deals with the issue of suffering and death particularly in chapters 11 and 21. You will read how He teaches by His own life and example what life is all about, and how we can know a close friendship with God. As with any other book, though, I recommend starting at the beginning of John's Gospel and reading through to the end. As you read ask God to reveal Himself to you.

However, I have selected from various parts of the Bible, passages which I trust will be of help at this difficult time.

Psalm 25:14-21
The secret of the LORD is with those who fear Him, and He will show them His covenant. My eyes are ever toward the LORD, for He shall pluck my feet out of the net. Turn Yourself to me, and have mercy on me, for I am desolate and afflicted. The troubles of my heart have enlarged; bring me out of my distresses! Look on my affliction and

my pain, and forgive all my sins. Consider my enemies, for they are many; and they hate me with cruel hatred. Keep my soul, and deliver me; let me not be ashamed, for I put my trust in You. Let integrity and uprightness preserve me, for I wait for You.

Lamentations 3:18-24
And I said, "My strength and my hope have perished from the LORD." Remember my affliction and roaming, the wormwood and the gall. My soul still remembers and sinks within me. This I recall to my mind, therefore I have hope. Through the LORD's mercies we are not consumed, because His compassions fail not. They are new every morning; great is Your faithfulness. "The LORD is my portion," says my soul, "Therefore I hope in Him!"

Matthew 6:25-34
"Therefore I say to you, do not worry about your life, what you will eat or what you will drink; nor about your body, what you will put on. Is not life more than food and the body more than clothing? Look at the birds of the air, for they neither sow nor reap nor gather into barns; yet your heavenly Father feeds them. Are you not of more value than they? Which of you by worrying can add one cubit to his stature? So why do you worry about clothing? Consider the lilies of the field, how they grow: they neither toil nor spin; and yet I say to you that even Solomon in all his glory was not arrayed like one of these. Now if God so clothes the grass of the field, which today is, and tomorrow is thrown into the oven, will He not much more clothe you, O you of

little faith? Therefore do not worry, saying, 'What shall we eat?' or 'What shall we drink?' or 'What shall we wear?' For after all these things the Gentiles seek. For your heavenly Father knows that you need all these things. But seek first the kingdom of God and His righteousness, and all these things shall be added to you. Therefore do not worry about tomorrow, for tomorrow will worry about its own things. Sufficient for the day is its own trouble.

Psalm 36:5-9
Your mercy, O LORD, is in the heavens; your faithfulness reaches to the clouds. Your righteousness is like the great mountains; your judgments are a great deep; O LORD, You preserve man and beast. How precious is Your loving-kindness, O God! Therefore the children of men put their trust under the shadow of Your wings. They are abundantly satisfied with the fullness of Your house, and You give them drink from the river of Your pleasures. For with You is the fountain of life; in Your light we see light.

John 3:16-21
"For God so loved the world that He gave His only begotten Son, that whoever believes in Him should not perish but have everlasting life. For God did not send His Son into the world to condemn the world, but that the world through Him might be saved. He who believes in Him is not condemned; but he who does not believe is condemned already, because he has not believed in the name of the only begotten Son of God. And this is the condemnation, that the light has come into the world, and men loved

darkness rather than light, because their deeds were evil. For everyone practising evil hates the light and does not come to the light, lest his deeds should be exposed. But he who does the truth comes to the light, that his deeds may be clearly seen, that they have been done in God."

John 11:25-26
Jesus said to her, "I am the resurrection and the life. He who believes in Me, though he may die, he shall live. And whoever lives and believes in Me shall never die. Do you believe this?"

Psalm 23:1-6
The LORD is my shepherd; I shall not want. He makes me to lie down in green pastures; he leads me beside the still waters. He restores my soul; he leads me in the paths of righteousness for His name's sake. Yea, though I walk through the valley of the shadow of death, I will fear no evil; for You are with me; your rod and Your staff, they comfort me.

You prepare a table before me in the presence of my enemies; you anoint my head with oil; my cup runs over. Surely goodness and mercy shall follow me all the days of my life; and I will dwell in the house of the LORD forever.

Also by Roger Carswell
Blessed are the dead who die in the Lord

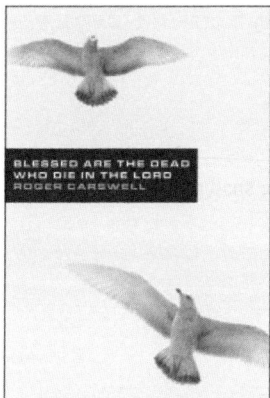

In the Book of Revelation, John, the author, describes how seven angels are sent to explain what is happening. One of these seven says, "Blessed are the dead who die in the Lord, from now on." God, the Holy Spirit, reinforces this with the words, "Yes, they will rest from their labours, for their deeds will follow them."

So the New Testament that begins with Jesus' Beatitudes, or blessings, ends with blessings for God's people. Although the words were written for those who die in the Great Tribulation, they have been an assurance that has encouraged all God's people who have stared death in the face.

Death is an enemy. It is a great destroyer. In a foul swoop death takes all the aspirations of a person, the dreams of their heart and the memories of the mind. Death severs the ties that bind a person to their loved ones. Death's work is relentless, cruel and merciless.

Yet God's verdict concerning His children who die in the Lord is that they are blessed of the Lord. How then, can that be?

May you be comforted by the words of this booklet as you face difficult times.

ISBN 1 85792 8946
ISBN 978-1-85792-894-5

Christian Focus Publications
publishes books for all ages

Our mission statement –
STAYING FAITHFUL

In dependence upon God we seek to help make His infallible Word, the Bible, relevant. Our aim is to ensure that the Lord Jesus Christ is presented as the only hope to obtain forgiveness of sin, live a useful life and look forward to heaven with Him.

REACHING OUT

Christ's last command requires us to reach out to our world with His gospel. We seek to help fulfill that by publishing books that point people towards Jesus and help them develop a Christ-like maturity. We aim to equip all levels of readers for life, work, ministry and mission.

Books in our adult range are published in three imprints.

Christian Focus contains popular works including biographies, commentaries, basic doctrine, and Christian living. Our children's books are also published in this imprint.

Mentor focuses on books written at a level suitable for Bible College and seminary students, pastors, and other serious readers. The imprint includes commentaries, doctrinal studies, examination of current issues, and church history.

Christian Heritage contains classic writings from the past.

For a free catalogue of all our titles, please write to
Christian Focus Publications, Ltd
Geanies House, Fearn,
Ross-shire, IV20 ITW, Scotland, United Kingdom
info@christianfocus.com
www.christianfocus.com